Buddha Box

Gretchen Mattox

New Issues Poetry & Prose

A Green Rose Book

New Issues Poetry & Prose
The College of Arts and Sciences
Western Michigan University
Kalamazoo, Michigan 49008

First Edition, 2004.

ISBN   1-930974-42-6 (paperbound)

Library of Congress Cataloging-in-Publication Data:
Mattox, Gretchen
Buddha Box/Gretchen Mattox
Library of Congress Control Number: 2003113931

Editors   Eric Hansen, David Dodd Lee,
                             Jonathan Pugh, Herbert Scott

Art Director   Tricia Hennessy
Designer   Aaron Carámbula
Production Manager   Paul Sizer
                             The Design Center, Department of Art
                             College of Fine Arts
                             Western Michigan University

Buddha Box

Gretchen Mattox

New Issues

WESTERN MICHIGAN UNIVERSITY

Also by Gretchen Mattox

Goodnight Architecture

Contents

III.

I.

Flying out from
the Great Buddha's nose
a swallow
—Issa

Buddha Box

no container for joy—all floor, all flood
pavement a cracked plate

no conception of well you couldn't hold

name the world to keep yourself from falling

not *falling*, misconception of metaphor

sightless lover
the bird's glory

even prayer to work against *not divine* enough why that decision?

to locate the wound was to locate your power

but joy also to locate your joy the being was not the body

the world as a container for joy

space　　dust　　　　　　　　　missing snow
that sensation of the world beneath a world—so foreign in a life of surfaces
palm trees lean like towers of Pisa　　　　　Staples sign　　grit of parking-lot sky
Shell Station, a single gull between the phone wires in motion, wings eyebrow signature

and Spirit calling you back, so that all day the world had weight
too rarified for　　breaking part of dusk absolute rendering of pink sunset over Playa del Rey
by breaking
the place where this world's dismantled
as lip to flame, flame in my belly, as the flame of words
little sparklers of prayer

all day wanting out and even death seemed less burdensome than desire

prayer was like a magnet drawing you to certain things
and not others, then even the dream, only a souvenir of the dream
it was nearly the solstice preparation for loss as much as beginnings

ants find the honey pot, they'll drown for it
in the pie tin filled with water, meant to detour, a moat surrounding the amber jar
and you, could you rise above the similar pull? one sensation after the next

always looking for the thing outside to make yourself known to yourself

Who is the lover? Are you both the lover and the loved?
Suffering, a wing (no bird), wound open to air—healing because all things tend toward.

Resist. You wanted your sorrow and your self (selfish) pity because maybe it justified limitations.
Because maybe it made you tired of the world.

All night—dreams like a window open somewhere;
close it! The past flying at you in exaggerated faces.
Who wants to look that closely at anything?

i.

Oh, diamond explosion of bliss and stillness, has the portal closed? Have you forgotten to find me here, waiting for you? Waiting. I have been waiting to stop having flying dreams that make no sense.

ii.

Every morning a new dream starts, so by evening the day dream and the night dream overlap, a blanket folded together. I live in the world as a body subject to the dream. Off in the distance in downtown L.A. a siren wails.

iii.

Walking. A pair of crows stare back—especially the one—propped on the fence post, glass-ink spill feather shimmer slow-motion wings, tentative fan (sitting so sure of himself almost refusing to fly).

Prayer made the mind wander—like being in love all the time.
Also the discouragement, because you felt undeserving. Hide out until you are perfect?
What kind of God do you have after all?

Shadows of consciousness in the [ego] glass house. Red grapes, cold and firm.

The part about surrender was the part where *rejoice* meant give up
passion play—stalled—no farther, as if love couldn't stop ringing

until clarity felt like emptiness, not filled *with* but open to

Flower-Seller, Lincoln Boulevard

Hurried stream of traffic. He stands in the cement island of safety
arms loaded with cellophane bundles: carnations rags on fire, tight
      fists of roses

across the street you can buy antiques and boats, whatever floats yours

Buy, buy, he's saying, all desperate gesture,
we are locked in our cars, in a hurry
to get where we are going, *home, work*

we are in a hurry to take what is ours to be taken
to make something of ourselves, to set our selves apart

and we don't have time for a flower-seller, his small bounty
however beautiful, and isn't it beautiful?

the color, the tender offering—call to love what is perishable
what isn't ours to keep

He'll be at it tomorrow, the next day, and someone will stop
roll down their window while the light is red

as if the moment was all that mattered
and pass the flower-seller five dollars

Unicorn Chinese Restaurant, Men Smoking

Out back in the alley two Chinese men in aprons and uniform hats
—white folded like newspaper boats—

light up by the trash bins off Lincoln, their cigarettes flash white
in an otherwise dim scape

greasy smells won ton something or other and all the other social ills
maybe it's good luck to go on *hoping*

how the dream of a better life stays buoyant like empty boats
        docked at the Marina
stumped as a child—how could anything so heavy *float?*

going through the day to day like that now

carried in spite of ourselves because we are human
and do not understand the meaning of grace

the passing glance of a lifetime streaked light in the ether

Cafe 50's,
Venice, California

alley pavement spider-cracked under theatrical streetlights
    throwing out yellow-pink megaphone light

you can walk through any dream back here, at *Princess Nails*
    (open late) Mexican girls chat and do it up with a pedi-mani
behind the black decorative grid of an iron door—only light gets
    in and out—

the neighborhood's not that good, the guy at the plant store will
    get you high
and across the street, gangs like a country of exile, still careful to
    take main, not side

there are three shadows of me, two out front, elongated bodies
    moving smoky as I walk, and one stubby me in back
    like the ongoing presence of the past

Lincoln Boulevard smear of light cars billboard promises there's more

love here than I ever thought possible, you have to strain to see it
past Rite Aid, some guy drunk on a bench, past the Frenchman
    gone crazy

who walks the streets beating his head with his fists

my waiter calls me *dear* and takes my order, The California
    Burger (turkey)

bright-red vinyl booths, spinning bar stools, kitsch movie posters—
    Cafe 50's fills up

Imitation of Water

As if the flight were interior not meant to manifest
Okay to float in the body   be *oceanic*

Rain all day   water rushing down the hill

rushing along the curb urban river rain pelting balcony
palm trees heaving up and down like chests sighing

clouds scarves over the hills you thought
star seeds falling on brick steps dissolved states of longing

Palm trees inverted question marks like hula skirts
the owl abated by distance

Does it all seem heavy, too much?

Fruit-Seller, Rose Avenue

hot October Sunday and he has bags of oranges, stacked like
    small cannonballs
the variegated watermelon, oval as fetal children

hard-luck stance against the brick wall
baseball cap over a towel sheikh-like and no takers

one sneaker against the wall and the other on the pavement
shade takes him in, hard angle of darkness actually visible

people pass on foot, on bikes, in cars
but he's disengaged done with *asking*

the difficult choices are the ones we don't make
like floating on your back in water

as if resignation is a higher option, but not today

he'll go home with maybe just enough or not
the margin of error narrow as two bodies pressed against one another

Ralph's, Lake and Lincoln,
Late Night

Hispanic checkout woman ignores my items while ringing them up.
Hey homey,
are those your tortillas? she says to the guy behind me.

No, he says. *You working late every night?*

Every night. Three kiwi (for a dollar) float on the conveyer belt
and the canned soup.

Shit, he says.

This invisibility goes deeper than customer service.
She imagines my life to be easy, the life she deserves.

I want to tell her, I know what it's like to be caught,
to do whatever is necessary.

Homey don't care. He has his six-pack and energy to flirt.
I hide behind *People* until the bag boy says *paper or plastic?*

half-smile as if the way we ignored each other

answers anger stilled as flies in the cold, no longer personal.

Alley, Indiana Avenue

Sparrows on the phone wires like abacus beads

over the Venice alley, mangled baby carriage garbage men can't take
(mysteriously bicycle-locked to chainlink fence)

black can line-up of issued trash and blue recycle bins—order for
the eye

Del Taco wrapper, a used condom like sausage casing

Some days there's beauty in it, the desolate no
one cares atmosphere—some care, plant roses, yellow angels in
their yard

Feng Shui bamboo to hide behind—hide from the less desirables
The known drug addict down the street has sworn off heroin

He might even try N.A., if not today, tomorrow
and what's a few drinks, everyone drinks or smokes

Venice 13 has tagged a garage with graffiti—modern hieroglyph

You can almost sense the Pacific in the way clouds form, boisterous
and absolute

Meanwhile, cars down Lincoln Boulevard *whizz*
fast as spit balls from the chute of a straw

Unwanted *Pennysaver,* Starbucks cup, the carpet-cleaning coupon tossed
each individual gesture—a consequential whole

Man in Clown Outfit

He's waving a plastic pointer, stiff flag enter lot here, parking
at the edge of Lincoln—bright-yellow clown suit with bold ruffles
    and floppy shoes
(the kind with stuffed toes) and from even a short distance he could be
anyone degraded selling *what?*, he could be, but he is a man,
    clearly Mexican,
underneath the nose that honks, a black mustache, illegal alien? probably.
Like the the girls in bikini tops and grass skirts outside casinos in
    Las Vegas,
who say, *Come get your free lei* (colored plastic wrap à la Hawaii), he does
what he's been told to do: on automatic, flag arm ticking like a metronome.

Underneath the painted smile is another expression—harder to place.
The urgency of traffic, who has time to care?
He takes his job seriously. On the way home, reverse route back,
he's still there waving, a swimmer treading water.

Can You Help Me?

it's desperate the way she looks—too tan, too blonde
to be hanging out at Costco asking for change

hard lined face, she's been at it awhile, drugs, poverty, who knows
what else

California sun gives false health
it's the inner death, the one we all avoid

that's taken her under, that takes you under
as you turn away "Not today"

But returning to the car, you hand her an orange,
the one you'd intended to eat for breakfast

and in the act for an instant you're not subject to flood of light and
shopping carts

morning sun too much to bear, honestly, too much

II.

The roaring waterfall
is the Buddha's golden mouth
—Su Tung-Po

Dead Dragonfly

Crumpled glider, body of thread bowtied on the stairs.

Did it make you feel defeated? *Lassitude.*

Here filling these syllables the expediency of song
is a day shaped by interruptions

Black moth—little girl's barrette.
The odd pair stayed on the stairs for days.

Coffin moth. In the way. Resigned.
For months you wanted to give up

the expediency of song, you couldn't take your own urgency
your own despondency

(be it light, be it open to light)
the instilled fears.

Churning and dying by self-propulsion.
as in the offertory fires of definition = crisis.

Then the agitation saying,
to claim the artistic self was to claim the mute self.

Residue

like when someone forgets where a sentence is going and trails off
        into silence
the former marriage, a parallel place

old angers like residue on glass:
last night for dinner, a tomato sliced into quarters
on the ceramic strawberry plates purchased in Sag Harbor

that spring of our final separation

I'm done judging, you say

sea-tossed anemic January honeymoon on St. George
Kool cigarettes piled high in a plate of ash and butts

around us the dunes changed like being inside the hourglass
and the TV that idiot box of local weather babbled degrees and tides

certain flowers to choose from, my little opiate no longer as if to
        acknowledge choice was to forfeit desire
but don't you get it drug of understanding I was *enveloped* and
        needed to be

Cold all the time the cold of dampness
the ocean hit the shore, volleyed with loss, tearing down the edges
        of things

we have each taken new lovers and think how long it's been

in the morning, the white shepherd, a stray in the neighborhood
wakes me up at dawn, passing ghost-like beneath my window
too wild to be caught, and starving

the moon is no mother

I am so tired of how the women are
their heads shrunken on the tips of sticks
and the light only they believe to be fire
why do they spend their sadness on trajectories?
the air is ill
silences live in it like passengers crammed in a car
here the mushrooms grow like toes in the dirt
how I hate the women's griefs
those sunken-eyed children thought to be lost
the ones with the grubbiest halos
the men always an angle in the distance
an exhumed cauliflower is a baby's brain
smoke exits the ashes
like hair undone before a mirror

See-Through Dream

In the dream we are all naked; a naked man mistakes me for a man.
"Are you wood or bush?"
"Wood," he answers, looking at my genitals.
"I am a woman," I insist,
closing the screen door behind me.

A dream where so much is see-through.

When I wake up, I feel more male, not *her;*
tired of the desire to make a home, make babies,
give love to God's creatures, defer power, be sweet.

All fire, ready to take and not worry if it offends.

Van Gogh's Ear

It was a cold ear, Vincent.
An insignificant sun dogged your heels.
Behind your easel, in another time, I worked a puzzle of a mountain scene.
Once, I put my ear to your breath and
let you take from me all the other moments.
I dreamed tropical birds became drinks with toothpick parasols,
which I offered to strangers,
strangers with a face like your face.
In one painting everything was auricular and yellow;
light superseded any self.
Eyes arranged in multitudes like battle stars offered no comfort.

Submission Watermark

watermark—a glass left too long and then removed

circle stain on wood—against the grain, how what I want to say
leaves me, an abandonment of self

words aren't everything

some said words stay like stains *the rage cloud building around you*
as if it were manly to pound, to demand submission

later a ladybug with no spots lands on my hand
all afternoon this is my comfort, she flies but not home

not home, the fire already out, the fire has already masterminded

devastation blackness against black, smoke, an afterthought
like what I want to say, but can't *enough*

Defiance

part defiance, part fatigue all summer long
the tomato plant—neglected

shriveled desert, frond-like, old peoples' skin

the crazy part was sublimation
it gave itself away, propagating round fiery balls
like blisters

brilliant sheen of fruit
I did not deserve—as if it were a matter of deserving
the life of hard soil, seeds planted that never offer much

while others unattended go wild

(you hate cats?)

In dream my ex-husband is heavier than I remember, like a wrestler (code for struggle I get it)—glad to see me.

Near the 14th Street subway in the park where the Farmers' Market is held, a stocky model all in white slides down a covered board intended to simulate snow—the seat of her pants wet like a kid's, thong showing through.

His apartment looks good. Jocko doesn't chase his cat—but the cat hides. (you hate cats?)

"I'll always love you," he says—"but I don't want to touch you."

My two Indian friends (from India) have just appeared and the three of them make dinner plans without me.

Anatomy of a Dress

Where the doll heads roll. Wonder as faith, knee-deep in sibilant
worry, a sleeve here, a sleeve there. Light over the hills, granular as
butterfly dust, thematic splitting. Did I dream the confessional?
Wasn't shame a shadow of protection? As in embryo, fishhook in
the womb? Maybe we carried each other? Maybe even forgiveness
is without resolution. Lines drawn as in don't go back. Lines drawn
as in who cares what name you give the other? By then I called out
to loss, the anemic capillaries, my own inability to ask for more.

Ruffled lip of sea froth (the feminine), to twirl all girly in the wind
of that making. Spin.

Furniture and neighborhoods are integral lost to motion.
The continent illumined by waste splits from the map.

Dialectic of Self and Sky

Love is moving through this the white space that approaches flatness.

In the whirlpool at the downtown Y.M.C.A. someone's loose hairs
    like a crippled spider.

Relax in the body. You could isolate the voice that said *grief* and
    the same voice
said *love* as in inhabit this day.

Disparaging—walking yourself in circles, walking around transitory
    happiness
because maybe you thought less of yourself for wanting it.

Paragraph of Skies

And in the hallway between states of consciousness, a stone temple, windows without glass and ocean light everywhere. I wanted to stay there. The neighbor appeared and gave the key, a key shaped like a fork.

Also the drowned flowers—lotus, maybe—left on the doorstep and the smell of loam.

House With No Path

Under an explosion of clouds, my mother and I walk across a
    dry riverbed.
The house is unfamiliar. We are in our astral bodies, learning love
    through loss.

Miles underscore my disbelief.
Spirit says, *there is magnitude in every inglorious moment.*

A woman on her hands and knees turns over stone after stone.
Afterwards, everything she touches becomes mollified, transformed.

In the middle of the desert, a girl with a bloody nose jumps rope.
The saguaro near an abandoned gas station catches fire. This is the
    alternate myth.

Wasn't it in another life I set out to find the very same house I am
    walking toward now?
I kept walking and walking, never getting any closer, but making
    continual effort.

Now with each step the house becomes displaced,
tilted against the sky as if viewed through a camera angle.

If there is a path, it is a path hewn with difficulty.
How many times have I had to die to get to this moment?

Spirit says, *forgiveness is acceptance,* and the souls fall into bodies,
one by one like skydivers oblivious to ground.

Story of Waiting

A strategic link of ants traverses the glass cylindrical bird feeder.
Failed venture of my longing, the sticky syrup like sap,
and all the while waiting.

Then: the hummingbird arrived, quiver of color and motion,

its green wings spinning faster than a playing card in a moving bike wheel,
that mock motor of childhood.

Do not despair. He hardly stayed—feeding (if he fed)
with a beak the length of his body.

The hope he brought, rush of light—all things of the world ending with loss.

Summer Oratorio

like astral butterflies landing on your fingers
all the while it's summer—weight and distraction of pleasures

the story, a good story appealing to triumph and song, myth
      reinventing itself
how the body breaks apart like dust, amen

theory: wizened branch cut off from the plant to explain separation, amen

bright disquieting silence and all the constellations molecular pinwheels
the world an inverse of itself, air like water, water like air

morning glory, little stars flashing on the hillside
neon purple / blue peacock feather eyes

sparrows fly through the seconds like darts,
wings—arms rotating in exercise class only faster

like as a child you turned into a torpedo underwater
that was *delightful (filled with light)*

Breast Cancer

for Chris and John

You held your cup, crossed the carpet and not one drop spilled.
Nothing broke—no sound cracks arrangement set.

The task was to keep living various clays of earth.
How *love* halted in you like a stopper in a bottle.

Frantic cellular mushroom the way one cloud builds sky,
rummage behind the skin / wall who would think to look?

Like playing the drunkard's game, sobriety line
you could walk it recite the alphabet that was *metaphor* only.

I wanted the field free and clear gesture of sisterly my brother loves you.
Irony: you had knockers, not the athletic boyish type of our mother.

Now we don't care we want your life we want the fight in you to win.
Who drew the line fed wrong info glitch of signals medical slant
        spiritual hassle;

we have faith but doesn't being careful count?

Nikki

i.

Light spreads across the sky inside me. A baby grows in furious divides (of actual fire radiance). It's about forgiveness and the ways in which we will inevitably fail each other. Some nausea. So I make pancakes (even the dog sleeps, ignoring the bang of pots) exclamation points of sound. Climb back into the pre-dawn bed, thinking of *you*.

ii.

I am my same self carrying you, flutter of cells worry want your heart to be, self-same replica and yet all yours until the undulation, a prayer flung past the subtle boundary between my desire for you and your desire for life.

iii.

love takes over fear, love parts the dream in halves and all are fed—

The cypress trees are inky towers in the just-dawn—light metallic with chill and a neighbor warms up a car engine down the hill. I was prepared to tell you all about darkness, but instead this, the vast welcome of the heart, the heart repeating itself beat by beat.

Nikki

after you went away, went back into the ether, still unformed, still
more consciousness than body—

Conjecture like wind animating leaves, the immediacy of certain
dreams while others remain idea-seeds. I was lonelier than I ever
thought possible.

Nikki

grief spills into the stillness of this   *I was well*   *deep invert*
   you, hum-bird bloody   *slipped between my legs in the*
shower soap-like   *and I held you, the piece of you, not human, really,*
   thumb-sized connective clot

nothing to recognize in the dream we lived together for nine weeks

like graphic backside of an eye

Nikki

my *phantom* fetus, cellular cloud—dreamed

garnet globular spill, wet trail out of the body, this grief without room
    for transgression

blood-jam from some remote region of being
beginnings made and left like the holding of hands *building the steeple*

and then collapse to touch again, I'll hold you
in that shadow world, too rarified for loss,

where matter dreamed—dissolves

Nikki

to this: my period like red storm *clouds* building and building until
      I remembered you [baby], the abstract of you, tunnel of light
          inside me,

cave closed off again—
      dark [fear] with stalagmites never meant to see light, the
          diminishing echo *mother* circling
like a wheel of sound getting smaller and smaller

thusly I had had it and wanted to break something that wouldn't matter
like a mismatched bowl or an empty bottle and watch the icicle splinters
bomb light and glass—
      a weight, all that weight dropped

Nikki

There is wonder. I pick oranges off the tree, reach high, stretching
    all the way inside.
If you'd stayed, I would have shown you this, the bounty of life;

blue sky in late December, oranges heavy as breasts, the unaccountable
    losses,
the speechless gifts.

III.

Altar for Inconstancy

you had to swim across the indoor pool and take an underwater elevator filled with water, a moving tank of water, glass, no air, only water and then the elevator stopped on the second floor, which turned into a regular restaurant, a place where couples leaned over the bar and all over each other. it was like Vegas. it was like another planet.

make the goal blue and the dream white. your rage—redundant.

one question enclosed in a body of water, enclosed in the body.

Sister Pilot

two kinds of birth opposing birth and the sentence stops there. to
be hidden at what cost because the presumed darkness kept you safe.
face of scars and damage dark cost. in one version the cost of self-
preservation was darkness, barefoot and alone in the snow village,
turning to strangers and strangers turning to you, shining your own
brightness back at you, new resonance.

O want—always more, always more than the world can give. the
body less than perfect flame, brightness lifting me out of the dark high
above nothing.

this is the blue (black) morning rising like Plath's contusion. she rang in
you, sister pilot cheater perfect wounded one Greek and dead.

by *morning* you meant not actual but allegorical.

I do love you but not in the way you want to be loved.

brightness lifting you even though you did not want to be lifted
escape promise, escape from what truth, *your own inevitable brightness.*

*you could project the body into the tree, you could lift the body with
only desire—a little elfish.*

and when night came, a helicopter circled Dodger Stadium like a sluggish
star, the dark opened spaces

let you bleed a little, forgive yourself for wanting perfection.

UnBelievable Heat,
Mother Wound

learned to use jealousy against myself on behalf of others so it helps
      that I can see your face from here,
a little disrupted, a milky-slur recited a couple of times before
      anonymous weather

unbelievable heat mother wound like an artificial fire

roar of two songs playing in one dream but I can't sing both at once
how to sing both at once? and see the point
of fire too small for the warming of hands but bright enough downwind
      to blind, bright enough to warn

large enough in the distance to hold many lives

I let it stay open mother / wound. I let whatever was in me that still
      needed you, need.
it was the wolf dream: *when she was five she dreamed over and over*
      she was being chased by wolves.

the wolves slept under my bed. wolf / mother. even writing this I hear
      the dogs / coyotes howl
over the hill. I hear their baleful wail of loss, where women turn
      against each other to survive.

Triptych: Falling Away

Parsley Lovers' Bisque

I ordered the lobster parsley lovers' bisque but was eating clear broth with
wide flat noodles.
"Whatever," said my mother. Whatever? Centuries of division like a hot
key in my hand. The noodles were the noodles of childhood.

the odd thing was I liked the clear broth, not the noodles, but the clear
broth was soothing like a cool palm to the forehead.

What the Earth Gave

such calloused insistence, I wanted the *bitterest* lemon the tree in a shower
of white petals as I took more than I needed, the ones out of reach.

calla lilies stiff like wearing good clothes to play in the yard.

yield, yield, I relented until the lemon tasted not sweet but *desirable* like
what I'd wanted all along without knowing it.

Bee Garden

garden sparse, extremely sunny, some bushes like interior structures
of the mind, a desert but still teeming with life and predominantly yellow.
a place without clear boundaries, a feminine place. like late-july mid-
morning when the volume of light intensifies drowsiness.

the bees are inferred but not seen. those seen, a few like chalk marks on
the board going between the bushes. the work is exactness. you carry the
bee garden inside; it is as actual as it is imagined.

Consensual Silence

in the dream I fear men but say nothing—reduction of disagreement—
    self with self and not the world
at large, two spiders—bodies bulbous as cocktail onions hang from
    the shelves
like the consensual silence inside me—

                    small girl, small girl, girl
whose only infraction is *being in the way of* that rage

later: the world like a bright jewel, rain on branch—
dropped

Jubilate Agno

—after Christopher Smart

For his divine click licking lap of the tongue whether the water is fresh or not.

For his discriminating palate and preference for butter over avocado as well as his keen interest in carrots (if diced bite-sized and a love of grapes) expressed with the rapt attention of the truly devoted, a devotee of begging and longing for any intended payoff, even crumbs count.

The way desire overtakes his dogliness and he focuses without interruption, hoping for a single grape, as if the grape, small globe, were the world itself.

For his bear-claw paws and the way his tired head fits between them, more regal than the lion statues at the New York City Public Library. His dignity resides in his paws, the way he carries them with total acceptance.

For the way he wakes up each morning with an old fluorescent tennis ball hanging out of his mouth like a cigar.

For the way he gives the sleeping body (myself or another) the fish eye, sitting patiently, saying please rise soon and take me on my walk.

For the way he increases his tactics if ignored, moving from fish eye to the paw.

For the way his paws demand, *paw, paw* and express what he can't say with words.

For his pig belly, baby belly, baby-soft nuzzle hairs on his tummy and how all four paws go limp in the air above him and his ability to doze off in ecstasy if petted long enough.

For his old man's snore, loud as a person's, really, if he's zonked out enough and in cocker spaniel dream land.

For his loneliest dog on earth wail whenever he gets left, for the way his loneliest dog on earth wail can be heard from the street, as if he is being tortured by an anguish nothing can touch.

The wail of ancestry, a little wolf bay, a little wild, and utterly human, a human utterance of abandonment, *don't leave me.*

For the way one small dog can take up a king-sized bed.

For the ways in which he expresses jealousy toward people and other animals; his sad eyes, his ability to muscle his way in, *me first.*

For the ways in which he shows up during sex, ready to participate, for accepting his banishment to a corner of the room while the people do what the people do.

For the ways in which he returns to the bed as soon as he can to join in, to not be left out.

For how he falls asleep at the end of the day, going limp in my arms, a pact of trust between us.

For how he saved my life when I didn't believe in love anymore. For Jocko, from John as in St. John, meaning God is good.

For Jocko from the pound, for Jocko who got left by someone who didn't want his demands anymore, his bark at trouble and danger (broadly defined as anyone new). His tough guy, I don't like men stance that had to be healed, that was healed by men who taught him to love, by men who taught me love by loving Jocko.

For the time he found a frozen elk skin in the Colorado mountains and appeared with his prize, stiff as a two by four and larger than his body. He carried the elk skin and smiled, a dog smile as if to show me his luck. The way he ran off so I wouldn't take it from him.

For his delight in rooting, the mock biting of, the snout digging into the pillow, the body slam against my body, the love mouthing, the playful snuggle that ends in rest.

For how he makes a nest, dragging the blanket between his teeth, digging at the bed as if he were digging a hole, and the circling circle, the attempt to find comfort, to reason with comfort.

For his love of pancakes and chocolates and his iron stomach. The way he ate a pound of chocolate from the airport in Frankfurt without getting sick. For the way he raided the Valentine's Day heart and left a box filled with empty chocolate papers.

For his God-given little dog body, the long dog ears that drag, the freckle-colored spots on his nose, his little stub tail, his docked tail that can do a happy circle, a little propeller, wind-up wind fan of delight that says *I am happy. I love.*

Looking for Work

in class someone said, "I think of artists as being like doves." and she held
her hand in a cup, *protective* "you have to be careful or they'll fly off."

it was beautiful. we agreed the image was beautiful as she opened her
hands, released them, the imaginary release. someone else said, "Kate
Chopin's *The Awakening* was banned. they considered it pornographic."

and someone else said, "Edgar Allen Poe married his fourteen-year-old
cousin." the momentum continued until we had them around us,
Hemingway, Chopin, Faulkner.

later the image: *doves*. fog light milky through palm trees, fertile body lit
resin sparkling like a pulse, as if *symbols* embodied a release more actual.

memory of doves on the fire escape in New York City years ago;
how they huddled and cooed, made sounds like *wind* whistled into
Peruvian clay pots.

how the shadows wreck us and poetry, a kind of bird you learn to hold

and whatever the cost, well, that was just life being life, the bird flying off
because you weren't meant to understand, not for long, not definitively.

Work

He stands between opposing traffic wearing the cardboard sign
  like a sandwich;
cartoonish red arrow pointing—*New Apartments, Free Rent*—
to brick villas, condo goes Mediterranean complete with balconies
  and ruffled awnings.

The traffic is spaced like irregular beads on a necklace—ever-moving
  urban river.

With just some slight adjustments the cardboard could stand on its own,
  be secured to something
other than this young boy who's *what?* come to America for the
  American dream

but doesn't speak the language yet or his papers aren't here and
  maybe never will be.

It's that terrible joke about *man's inhumanity to man.*
How many like me will pass and notice him, feel—empathy, anger, pity—

but move on in their cars—do nothing?

Alte Romerstrasse, Dachau, 2001

"Out of the depths I cry to you, O God . . ."
—Psalm 130, *Hebrew Bible*

the worst part was not the pictures of men in jail-suits, hands tied
        behind their backs,
hung from the wrists, dangling inverted—

that dislocates your shoulders, said my mother; or the accounts of
        medical experimentation—
another man's scalp cut off so as tourists we saw his cranial matter,
        wormy, bloodless bald monk's cap

and still more, a floating woman—clothed, in a tank filled with
        cold water

an experiment designed to test the body's resistance to
        extreme temperatures

or the crematorium, empty—the un-noted dead, *this room was
        never used as an actual crematorium*
the trench where people were lined up and shot

the worst part was not the recessed eyes of the starving or the
        sleeping quarters like stalls
or that the Museum started with a history of the Nazi party
        and not an apology, not a prayer

In renovation, said the sign

how we couldn't find our balance, *this happened in your lifetime,*
I say to my mother and we are stunned with mutual denial—
        the ground beneath us opening up

as if the mouths of the dead want to speak in the dark, want the
        odd silence of *beautiful* spring
to shimmer like a vigil—not drug us with oblivion and light

we are cold in our coats and gloves, the leftover snow in patches
        across the ground
inside the Church of Reconciliation a few votives burn,
        little teacups of spirit

the worst part wasn't what was said, but what wasn't—how something
     so dark
could still live a little, part scar, part shame, entirely evil

how you had to listen hard to hear *history* above the blare of the present.

1. flying: a retrospective

ash marked bark from colorless fire like a blind marble how the
        quail so stupidly docile peck at the
hill
all colors on a gray continuum gray to further gray, Denmark at
        dusk—a perspective of alterations. I
didn't anticipate
having to defend malleable self with nothing but a show of
        twigs determination

then I dreamed red door where friends could come and go to let
        out the loneliness, desire the curve
of extended hills not meant to be touched SAID sad girl making
        stick circles

2. flying: a prayer

up and down the spine ride maybe water is a kind of luminary, clock
wind against the back, helping wind helping push push and then the
prayer was no longer *for* but to be shown a willingness

dead possum entrails like crushed carnations, an experiment in floral
dyes, how the white flowers drink the red food-colored water, dead
squirrel a little fur beret, nap of hair parted by wind, dead wind so
still I can hear myself think in many languages all of them sacred all
of them lies

3. flying: a lover

if it's about a fix it's about an out and you in the hole distaste your life
        can only put out a little flag of
hope
that has nothing to do with relief whoever they are with their vague
        promises forget them
forget it all if you can until the body made of bones shrinks like any
        aspect in the distance

don't need it not the place of conforming to what wasn't meant to be,
        bride of light, drink from heaven
not anyone's hand

4. flying: a requiem

garden ignored for two seasons read as process flowers almost sea
        anemones they seemed living pink
pained with their outpouring air thick as a seabed

beyond artificial sleep body *sleep on your own time* smile by smile
        actually petal by petal
private collective gift—endless insistence

how were you swayed? rolled inside yourself until the weight of earth
        could no longer hold you

5. flying: the breaking of names

to sing was to claim doubt even in the abstract it seemed wrong
        once and false later—
so faced with the ability to choose a *version*

I chose the vagaries of wings like tents grounded for storm,
        heaped ash—almost motionless
no matter what *no matter what*

but there was motion *is it worth telling lies for?* the breaking of
        names [ego]
pain meant letting go of who you were *supposed* to be

I Love This Poor Life 4 Real

where the PCH opens up—view of ocean, flat continence
        gulls dip amusement park high wire fall in complete control
hard to believe any blue so strong isn't solid
in this tunnel of traffic, Egyptian-like the tomb gives way to light

wink red brakes, we're stalled again and who knows why—
        today no particular joy

I do what's in front of me to do, accept what I've been given as
what I've been given how that differs from getting what you want
technicalities still worth arguing

it's stop and go all the way, a little journey humor

graffiti message on neighboring wall: I love this poor life 4 real

the choice we're given to leave or take

Notes

The *nikki* is a Japanese literary form of prose mixed with poetry. It is generally translated as "diary." It was popular with female authors, from empresses to court servants. Abutsu-ni's *Izayoi Nikki* is one of the most popular from the Kamakura era, which lasted in Japan from 1186 to 1336.

In "I Love This Poor Life 4 Real," "PCH" refers to the Pacific Coast Highway—also called Highway 1, and renowned for its beauty. It follows the coastline of the Pacific Ocean down the western United States.

The works I relied on in this book are:

Ch'an Master Hsuan Hua. *Sutra in Forty-Two Sections*. San Francisco: Buddhist Text Translation Society, 1977.

Garvey, Mark. *Searching for Mary*. New York: Penguin Putnam, 1998.

Mills, Laurence-Khantipalo. *Jewels Within the Heart*. Thailand: Silkworm Books, 1999.

Ellinger, Herbert. *The Basics: Buddhism*. Trans. John Bowden from the German *Buddhismus* published 1988 in the *kurz und bundig* series. London: SCM Press, 1996.

Thurman, Robert. *Inside Tibetan Buddhism*. San Francisco: CollinsPublishers, a division of HarperCollins, 1995.

Lambdin, Robert Thomas and Cooner Lambdin, Laura, edited by. *Encyclopedia of Medieval Literature*. Westport, Connecticut: Greenwood Press, 2000.

Hanson, Kenneth. *Words of Light*. Council Oaks Books, 2000.

Acknowledgments

Many thanks to the editors of the following magazines in which these poems first appeared, some of them in different versions:

Fish Drum: "Buddha Box (no container for joy)," "Buddha Box (space)," "Buddha Box (prayer was like a magnet)," "Buddha Box (Who is the lover?)," "Buddha Box (Oh, diamond explosion)," "Buddha Box (Prayer made the mind wander)"

Quarterly West: "Residue"

Rivendell: "Flower-Seller, Lincoln Boulevard," "Unicorn Chinese Restaurant, Men Smoking"

Shade: "the moon is no mother," "Can You Help Me?," "Ralph's, Lake and Lincoln, Late Night," "Alley, Indiana Avenue," "Alte Rommerstrasse, Dachau, 2001," "Consensual Silence," "(you hate cats?)," "See-Through Dream"

Slope: "Sister Pilot," "UnBelievable Heat, Mother Wound," "Jubilate Agno," "Looking for Work"

I would like to thank David Dodd Lee for giving me the gumption to give my all; my family for their ramparts of love; dear Jocko and sweet Pilar; as well as my friendships, writerly and otherwise, that offer ongoing sustenance in the face of change. A special thank-you to: Victoria Andaházy, Maro Chermayeff, Nicole Cooley, Deborah Landau, Dana Levin, Amy Schroeder, and Heidi Vogel.

photo by Muriel Mutzel

Gretchen Mattox has been a fellow at the Edward Albee Foundation,
the Virginia Center for the Creative Arts, and Yaddo. She has lived
in numerous places, including Denver, Provincetown, and New
York City, and currently resides in Los Angeles. She is the author
of *Goodnight Architecture.*

New Issues Poetry & Prose

Editor, Herbert Scott

Vito Aiuto, *Self-Portrait as Jerry Quarry*
James Armstrong, *Monument In A Summer Hat*
Claire Bateman, *Clumsy*
Michael Burkard, *Pennsylvania Collection Agency*
Christopher Bursk, *Ovid at Fifteen*
Anthony Butts, *Fifth Season*
Anthony Butts, *Little Low Heaven*
Kevin Cantwell, *Something Black in the Green Part of Your Eye*
Gladys Cardiff, *A Bare Unpainted Table*
Kevin Clark, *In the Evening of No Warning*
Cynie Cory, *American Girl*
Jim Daniels, *Night with Drive-By Shooting Stars*
Joseph Featherstone, *Brace's Cove*
Lisa Fishman, *The Deep Heart's Core Is a Suitcase*
Robert Grunst, *The Smallest Bird in North America*
Paul Guest, *The Resurrection of the Body and the Ruin of the World*
Robert Haight, *Emergences and Spinner Falls*
Mark Halperin, *Time as Distance*
Myronn Hardy, *Approaching the Center*
Brian Henry, *Graft*
Edward Haworth Hoeppner, *Rain Through High Windows*
Cynthia Hogue, *Flux*
Christine Hume, *Alaskaphrenia*
Janet Kauffman, *Rot* (fiction)
Josie Kearns, *New Numbers*
Maurice Kilwein Guevara, *Autobiography of So-and-so: Poems in Prose*
Ruth Ellen Kocher, *When the Moon Knows You're Wandering*
Ruth Ellen Kocher, *One Girl Babylon*
Gerry LaFemina, *The Window Facing Winter*
Steve Langan, *Freezing*
Lance Larsen, *Erasable Walls*
David Dodd Lee, *Abrupt Rural*
David Dodd Lee, *Downsides of Fish Culture*
M.L. Liebler, *The Moon a Box*
Deanne Lundin, *The Ginseng Hunter's Notebook*
Joy Manesiotis, *They Sing to Her Bones*
Sarah Mangold, *Household Mechanics*
Gail Martin, *The Hourglass Heart*
David Marlatt, *A Hog Slaughtering Woman*
Louise Mathias, *Lark Apprentice*
Gretchen Mattox, *Buddha Box*
Gretchen Mattox, *Goodnight Architecture*
Paula McLain, *Less of Her*
Sarah Messer, *Bandit Letters*